Having A Wonderful Time At Whitley Bay

A selective, subjective and highly personal social history of Whitley Bay, illustrated where appropriate with postcards

Water Chute and Figure Eight Railway, Whitley Bay

by Bill Mood

Also available from Summerhill Books

Glimpses of Tynemouth, Cullercoats & Whitley Bay

Glimpses of Old North Shields

North Shields – The Bombing of a Town

Wallsend Best – A Personal Experience of the Rising Sun Colliery

The publishers would like to thank George Nairn for supplying the postcards on pages 6, 8 (top), 11 (top), 13 (bottom) and page 36 (bottom).

Copyright Bill Mood 2010

First published in 2010 by

Summerhill Books
PO Box 1210
Newcastle-upon-Tyne
NE99 4AH

Email: andrew_clark@hotmail.co.uk

ISBN: 978-1-906721-25-1

Printed by: CVN Print Ltd, Maxwell Street, South Shields

Introduction

Hi, and welcome to my Dad's book.

It all started when, rooting around a junk stall, I found a postcard of Whitley Bay. I showed it to Dad and got "I remember that!" and a story about something on the card. A little while later and the same thing happened, except that this time it was "I don't remember that!" and after a trip by him to the local study centre there would be another bunch of reminiscences.

Gradually, I started to hear stories of Whitley Bay that had never surfaced in the previous 40-odd years. I suggested to him that maybe he should record all of this, and in one month-long splurge he wrote the text of the book.

That was over ten years ago. Since then there have been periods of doing nothing about the book, interspersed with talking to the wrong people, until finally I met up with publisher Andrew Clark - and here we are with a material item, a real book, properly printed and published and everything.

It is not an exhaustive piece of research, nor is it a chronological history. Rather, it is the story of what it was like to grow up in a town in its heyday, in the golden era of the seaside resort. We have used postcards to illustrate the book, mostly from that era. I hope you enjoy it as much as we have enjoyed the process of putting it together.

Mike Mood
March, 2010

Historians will tell you that the whole of the Whitley Bay area was only sparsely populated until relatively recently. It has been covered at various times with coal and ironstone mines, a couple of brickworks, the magnesian limestone quarry and lime kilns, a brewery or two and the salt pans at Cullercoats, and all this activity spread to that other hive of industry and port at Seaton Sluice. It is hard to imagine now; by 1850 the industry had worked out at Whitley Bay (the small lump on the links near the war memorial is spoil from an ironstone working) and in the 1860s the builders started to develop the area which had been opened up

AERIAL VIEW OF WHITLEY BAY   59

by the railways. The Blyth and Tyne Railway and the lines from Newcastle made the area available for people to live in and enjoy a better life than crowded together in Newcastle. You can see the slow start from Cullercoats northwards where many of the

The Vicarage, Whitley Bay.

older houses have dates on them but since my family came here in March 1935 little has changed between Cullercoats and the cemetery. The area behind Whitley Bay station and the Broadway was being built up in the late '30s and the Whitley Lodge area in the 1950s, but otherwise only small vacant plots have been built on over the years. I look back at these cards with nostalgia, although of course many of them are from a time before I was born. However, my friends' parents could talk about their childhood when a lot of central Whitley Bay was fields and market gardens. The Vicarage on Park View (TESCO now) had gone by 1931 and I can only remember three major building changes: the old school at the corner of Norham Road was demolished and the Telephone Exchange and Hotspur Hall eventually erected on the site, the bus station was built and relatively recently the expansion of Woolworths onto the old council buildings.

Whitley Bay was never on the scale of Blackpool or even Scarborough but it was the popular lung of Tyneside and grew from the 1880s as a place to go to for a pleasant stroll on the Esplanade or promenades which were being built to accommodate the crowds that came. All were well dressed and indeed this was part of the ritual, to dress up after working hard all week in your "work" clothes. The boarding houses sprang up and the visitors came to stay. Board Residence signs were discreetly placed in windows and also "apartment" signs – this meant "room only – bring your own food" which the landlady would cook. After World War I the

The Promenade, Whitley Bay.

season became more commercialised as more people could afford holidays. Even though times were hard and the depression of 1930-35 took place, paid holidays came into being in the mid 1930s, and the 1920s and 1930s were the heyday of Whitley Bay as a holiday resort. It tried hard to re-establish itself after World War II but by the mid 1960s any pretence had gone. The Pierrots or summer shows stopped, there was no swimming pool (until the 1970s) and the long-standing discussion of having a pier was no longer a topic of conversation, so Whitley Bay as a resort gave way to Benidorm and the guaranteed sunshine. To build a pier needs an Act of Parliament which we had but it needed to be reviewed until the pier was actually built and as far as I know the bill lapsed without use. The original company had gone bankrupt many years before.

CATLIN'S ROYAL PIERROTS, WHITLEY BAY, 1906.

What do I really remember of my childhood? It ended to a large extent with the war which changed everything and by the time it was over I was no longer a child and had sailed the seas and been sunk and rescued and once even fired an Oerlikon gun at a German plane. I hasten to add that my war whilst bad enough was in no way so horrific as a front line soldier's and our home although damaged by bombs was not destroyed as others were. The war gets blamed for so many things but it was a major milestone to our generation. So many things that were there before the war disappeared never to return but as it lasted six years there would have been some change anyway as we all want progress in our living conditions. It just seems a pity that just when money was more plentiful and new shops were opening in 1938/39 like Arthur's Oyster Bar they then closed for ever. Also Tyne Taxis had started in Monkseaton next to Kelly's DIY. They had a fleet of beige and brown taxis and similar livery colours for the uniformed chauffeurs; they looked very smart and of course taxis were only for special occasions. Very few people used them on a daily basis – how could they call them? Only by public telephone boxes, as not many private homes had telephones.

Before we came to Whitley Bay we lived at 46, Shaftsbury Crescent, Sunderland. This was in the Humbledon Hill council estate built in the early 1920s. It is still in my opinion a nicely built estate; some of the houses on the main road have timbered elevations which gives them some pretence to grander living. The rooms were small and the bathroom, kitchen and lavatory were all on the ground floor to save piping! We had hot water, electricity and gas, plenty of windows and quite a large back garden to grow vegetables – all good, clean and healthy and a far cry from the properties where my parents grew up and where four of my uncles and aunts died from TB.

RIVER WEAR FROM WEAR BRIDGE, SUNDERLAND.

We sometimes walked through the fields to Tunstall Hills and if we walked the other way we passed Barnes Park school where my father and his sisters and I in turn attended, and in a little while we reached Eden House Road, where I was born and where my grandparents still lived. It was only an upstairs flat with gas light, but I liked the warm yellow glow and in winter they always had crisp celery and Wensleydale cheese. They had a motor bike and side car and roamed over Durham and Yorkshire but they were a quiet couple and, after losing two daughters, very sad people who died young. Those were the times and nothing unusual, but it would not happen now. What else do I remember of those early days? We had an annual holiday until I was four and I have memories of being on a farm near Whitby. My baby sitters were all single ladies who should have been married but whose men were killed in Flanders. They used to read the Rainbow Annual to me and "Gloops" and "Rag Tag and Bobtail".

Once a Co-op dairy milk cart fell over in the next street, Shrewsbury Crescent, where there was a slope; the road was icy and the poor horse fell over. What a commotion! We all watched the horse frantically trying to regain its footing but it was trapped in the shafts and had to be cut free. We never knew the outcome as the local bobby who lived nearby came out and chased us all away. He was the law and all obeyed him. I also remember the stigma of receiving free school milk. This had only just started at schools in Sunderland to help rid the population of rickets and if your father was out of work the milk was free; we were not allowed to drink it with the others, but had to leave the class as a group, get our free milk, drink it, return the bottle to a teacher and say thank you. Times have changed!

Times were hard in the early 1930s, the shipyards closed and my father was out of work for almost four years. We had first come to Whitley Bay on summer holidays in 1930 to stay with my mother's school friend Jenny Clark who lived at the top of Holly Avenue and whose husband owned the newsagent on Park View (this is still there). With their help it was decided that we would live in Whitley Bay so that my mother could take in visitors during the summer season to make some money and my father was to work in Laidlers fish shop. The thought of this filled him with horror and "luckily" Herr Hitler started to bang the drum; the shipyard suddenly had work once

more and my father returned to work in the William Doxford's shipyard where he had started work in 1914 and where he stayed until 1965. (We always called the German leader Herr Hitler and most kids thought that was his name. The papers

only started to call him Adolf when pretence at being nice to Germany was dropped. Funny how fashion changes – now the use of forenames is correct, then it was being unduly familiar). Dad lived weekdays with his father (Grandmother died in 1934) and travelled back to Whitley Bay for the weekends. This continued for three years until my Grandfather died in 1937.

I went for one term only to Park Infants School, March-July 1935 in Miss Scott's class. Miss Bell was the head mistress, a very small lady with a wilting look and a sharp tongue, especially when trying to teach seven-year old girls to knit. At first I didn't know anyone and was a bit bolshie, so was caned three times. It was really a very large piece of dowel which was tapped on your hand but the experience was enough. At the end of the morning and afternoon sessions we had to line up into two

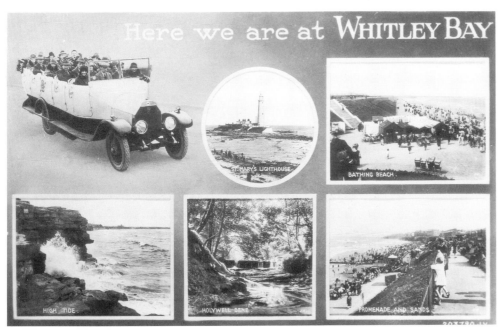

groups – those who had to cross Park View and those who had to cross Park Road, and a teacher had to see us across these roads. Apparently a child had been killed or injured and this was to prevent another accident. Coming from the large town of Sunderland

I thought this was rather beneath my dignity but we all had to go in convoy. It was during this time at the Park Infants that we were all taken to the sea-front to see the *Mauritania*, one of the grand old liners of the *Titanic* and *Lusitania* period. Built of course on the Tyne by Swan Hunter and Wigham Richardson and such was the local pride that we were taken to see the old lady on her way to her demise in a ship breaker's yard in Scotland. I remember it as a fine day but very hazy and the ship which was all white was to me like a ghost gliding out of the hazy sea and sky. I remember thinking it was very sad; perhaps even then I had a feeling for ships which led me to sea when I was 16. The school dentist made

Cunard R.M.S. "MAURETANIA" PASSING DOWN THE RIVER TYNE
This ship holds all the Atlantic records, both Eastward and Westward, for highest speed and fastest passages.

Built by SWAN, HUNTER, & WIGHAM RICHARDSON LTD Wallsend-on-Tyne.

visits during this time in a travelling "caravan surgery" and I also remember small biplanes skywriting, usually soap powders like Persil and Rinso, which was quite a novelty then. Although I was only at the school for a short time Miss Bell, when in her retirement, often sat on a seat near the Park Lodge House and she always spoke to me for years after and seemed especially pleased with me when I donned a uniform.

I did not like Whitley Bay at first – this was March 1935 – no back garden, an outside loo, and only gaslight in the kitchen and no bathroom! However by June I had my first friend in Whitley Bay, called Billy Simpson (he and his family were killed in their house when German planes dropped mines by parachute which exploded in Ocean View) and we discovered the freedom of the beach and rocks, and roamed from Cullercoats to St Mary's Island.

In late spring 1935 on a warm June night Billy told me that there were newts at Curry's Point and we set off to get some with a jam jar! We had both become eight years old and considered ourselves capable. Walking along the sands, we collected driftwood (there always seemed to be lots of wood on the beach in those days) which we had to stash as it became too heavy to carry. We reached the large hollows at the shooting butts and tried and tried but the newts were too quick for us to catch. Disappointed, we set off for home and collected the wood. The darkening

WTB 3   WHITLEY BAY   Photo by J. F. LAWRENCE
THE LIGHTHOUSE, ST. MARY'S ISLAND

sky and tiredness made us dispose of the jam jars and then piece by piece the wood was dropped until, approaching civilisation, we saw the Ice Cream shops closing. To Billy's experienced eye this meant 10 pm and we raced home to find both Police and Fire Brigade had been mustered to look for us. Billy got a sore bottom from his father's belt – luckily my father was in Sunderland and so all I got was "wait till your dad gets home" but the weekend was a lifetime away and nothing happened.

In 1937, with a new friend Granville Wood, we discovered Holywell Dene. We used to load up my barrow with a tent, tins of baked beans and a bottle of Tizer and set off over the railway bridge, along the allotments path behind Deneholm and through the fields past Red House farm. Then we had to cross the railway line at Briardene, through the farmyard and down into the dene where the old Engine House was. We pitched a tent, lit a fire to cook our baked beans and roast potatoes. We had found a

rope which Ronnie Steel tied to a high branch and we swung on it and imitated Johnny Weissmuller's Tarzan. (Ronnie was the only one of us brave enough to climb the tree!) The old mill had not worked for twenty years but there were still two houses and one sold sweets and "pop". The dene, which is hardly used now, was well used in the 1930s although it had been an even more popular walking and picnic area pre-World War I.

So for five years Easter, Whitsun, Race week and the summer four weeks holidays were spent either on the beach, the rocks or Holywell Dene. October "blackberry week" was supposed to provide cheap labour for potato picking but I only ever used the week for blackberrying. We spent hours fishing or swimming at Table Rocks pool.

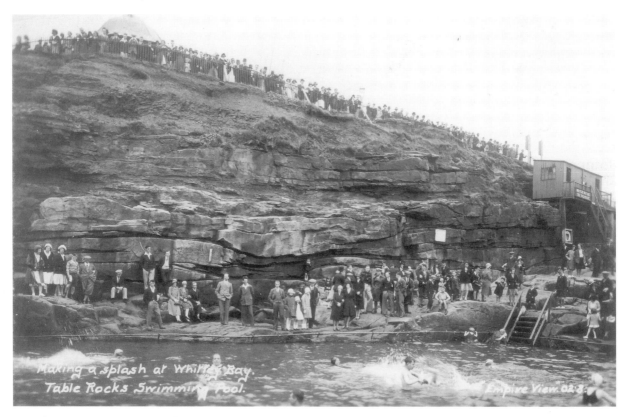

Making a splash at Whitley Bay.
Table Rocks Swimming Pool.
"Empire View" 02.8

False memory makes me think that all the summers were sunny and warm, and whilst the late 1930s were good I can also remember standing with teeth chattering and fingers devoid of blood trying to fasten my shirt buttons after swimming in the pool. Whilst my family were not well off, as an only child I always had toys – Meccano and a fabulous chemistry set which kept me busy during the winter. Later I made model aircraft and flew them on the Links. The interest in model planes was due to the war – Battle of Britain – and whilst I built and flew Kiel Kraft planes – Spitfires, Hurricanes, Gladiators etc – my big flier was just a model something like Lindbergh's plane which

flew the Atlantic, but it was a beauty. One day Ronnie Steel and I went to the little bump on the Links winding the propeller and elastic band as we walked. I set the plane off to fly to the Spanish City. A perfect flight, but the wind banked the plane and it disappeared over the promenade; with sagging jaw and trembling lips we saw it fly over the sands and out to sea. Fair stood the wind – but not for France! Round came the plane and landed on the hard sand as if piloted. Horrors! All the beach and lower prom were barricaded and barbed wired against invasion, but the beach was opened for one hour twice a day by a soldier on duty at Watts slope. We hurried down to beat

10

the incoming tide and luckily it was just time for the gate to be opened. The plane was rescued!

There were also the street gangs when we played around the street lights and in the back lanes on good nights. The very idea of back lanes and back yards is now scorned, but it produced a culture and had many advantages which are now lost and gone. Children played safely, there was always some housewife watching her youngest play on a clippie mat. We played "mount the cuddy" (below), and "tig" which gave us team spirit. We played marbles in the season, which taught us to count and whips and tops gave us dexterity. Gurds and hooks vied with tops and whips but were fading during the 1930s. I could never understand how it would be tops and whips and as if on command they would stop until next year and it was marbles or

hopscotch that was in favour or the old favourite skipping with all its different styles.

The girls dressed up in their mothers' old dresses, shoes and hats and paraded and showed off to the not very interested lads. Then they did handstands against the wall and showed off their knickers which must have all been in some social cause. All good clean innocent fun and a lot of it before the age of five which made it the nursery school of the day, so long as you heeded the dread warning of mams to keep away from the big drain (and so avoid diphtheria). However, this was all in the older parts and the larger houses and new estates had the back gardens to play in. Progress! There are also the avenues in some parts of Whitley Bay – no front road which gave more space to build houses for the working man, good artisans but who could not afford to ride in carriages so did not need a roadway. They made great play areas when I was a child. Now they are

"pedestrian precincts" and in vogue again and necessary as the back lanes are full of cars. Of course Whitley is far from alone in these changes and there are new games that children play. The terminology of children and of the local trades has gone with the effects of radio and television making us all one nation and very Americanised. Life was very parochial; you shopped, played and talked locally and "kept it all in the family". Events like Carling Sunday, we were taught, commemorated a ship loaded with Carling peas which had broken the siege of Newcastle by the Scots and saved the starving population. We used to chant "Carlin-Palm and Paste Egg" day anticipating Easter and the first holiday of the year. More coarsely, fathers used to say "Carlin Sunday, Fartin Monday"! I can't understand Paste Egg day, was it Pace (Peace) Day on Easter Sunday? North East words like "Tagarene Shop" – seamen and miners' shops which sold all the working clothes and tools – or "cuddy handed" for left handed people have gone out of use. It was never derogatory but was an affectionate term. In fact people who did have impediments like cleft palate or rickety limbs were protected by their "gang peers". Thankfully such disadvantages are corrected by doctors and surgeons and a better diet prevents many of yesterday's illnesses; the annual springtime scourge of measles, mumps, scarlet fever etc have been almost eradicated by Medicine. Thank heavens for real progress.

The summer season only lasted a few weeks in Whitley Bay. Visitors started in mid-June, these were older or retired people. July was busy because the Bradford-Leeds mills closed and people came from there (paid holidays started in the 1930s). Later came the Scottish mills towns, Peebles, Hawick,

Galashiels and hundreds came from Glasgow (more liberal drinking hours in Whitley Bay) but after the first week in August it slowed down and it was back to the older people, until first week in September when it tailed off completely. In all, ten weeks covered the season, six of these being busy, busy, busy. When a sign went up saying

THE NEW N.E.R. STATION WHITLEY BAY.

"Board Residence" or "Apartments", the Sanitary Inspector from the Whitley and Monkseaton Urban District Council came to see the premises and there had to be no more than 8 bottoms per lavatory seat.

I received lots of three-penny and six-penny coins, sometimes for playing with children of the visitors or for taking their luggage to the station on my bogey. After the first two years, when repeat bookings were being made, I used to go to the station to collect people and luggage – it was always the railway, never the bus. We used to have visitors from as far away as Sheffield, but also from as near as Cramlington. Whitley station was a very busy place pre-war. During "Scotch week" when the place was full of Scots, trains ran direct to Glasgow and there were excursions to many places but also the riverside line (now gone) took hundreds of workers to the shipyards from North Shields up to Walker and we used to go to the barriers at 5 to 5:30 pm to ask for cigarette cards. I saved many sets and put them in albums, but after I had gone to sea and with toys etc

being in short supply my mother gave them away. I rarely ventured to Monkseaton, one or two friends moved to new houses in West Monkseaton and I visited them on occasion but I knew very little of anything west of the railway line. There was no ice rink before 1950 and the hollow next to it which is now the cricket club was at one time an old quarry which the council then owned and which was used as a refuse tip. Huge red beetles started to breed there and they marched into the council houses over the road. There was an outcry, the tip was closed after being covered in soil and grass and the beetles or roaches disappeared. During the war the council tried to let the ground as allotments but the soil was thin and poor and it was not a success.

I used to go to Cullercoats more often but we were foreigners and all we did was swim and play. We did try to harpoon dabs and plaice which used to bask on the sand in shallow water. There were lots of boats at Cullercoats, only 6d to hire one for half an hour, 6d for a harpoon head and a 6 foot long bamboo but I never caught anything – I couldn't understand the parallax of seeing things through water and I always missed.

There are new houses at Cullercoats now but the old cottages were still there until the 1960s although the Cullercoats families had left for more affluent places by then. The cottages only had one room, with a bed in one corner, a table, 3 or 4 chairs and a rocking chair, and a kitchen range for heating and cooking. A small table usually stood outside the door from which they sold crabs, lobster and fish. The cobles went out at night and the fish were landed and cleaned and the shellfish boiled and onto the street being hawked by the women. They were all hard-working and manned the lifeboat and went to the Mission on Sundays; it was a real community and to some extent it still is, if you are one of the families.

My daily visit in that direction was to Rockliffe school where I went for my three junior school years from August 1935. There was no school for the expanding area of West Monkseaton so the children there attended Bygate School, children from that area attended Park School and in turn we in the Park School area attended Rockliffe. We usually walked along Esplanade Place through the cut in Victoria Avenue following the line of the old wagonway which used to take the coal and ironstone from the links and coastal area and the coal from the Churchill playing field pits to Cullercoats. In good weather we used the promenade, at least to come home. There were no school meals and I made the journey twice each way every day. When I had money I went along Whitley Road as it was by then called – all the individual names, Arcadia, Catherines Terrace, Regent Terrace, etc all joined up to become Whitley Road.

The Village, Whitley Bay.

We used to get our sweets at Websters (or Waggots, I can't remember the name) which was a small corner shop opposite the Rockliffe pub. A twist of newspaper filled with sweets (no weighing!) and then to Storey's to dream of buying a train set. One item of intense news was in about 1937 Steels the jewellers (later Collingwoods and then a video shop) was burgled. Some of the children from our school found the loot buried in a pile of building sand near to the Rockliffe pub. They were duly rewarded in a ceremony at school much to the envy of the rest of us. A letter from the Chief Constable and a savings certificate followed. "Virtue is its own reward" – oh boy, weren't those days simple.

Arcadia, Whitley Bay.

I had three teachers at Rockliffe School. Miss Hall was an old lady who must have been nearing retirement. Miss Robson taught the middle year. She was alright but sharp with her tongue and wore the same style of black dress which reached her ankles that was in fashion when she first became a teacher in pre-World War I days. We received a mug and half a day holiday for George V's Silver Jubilee, a prayer and two minutes shuffling silence when he died. We were in Miss Robson's when Edward VIII came and went, and sang ribald songs about Mrs Simpson without knowing why and then we were given a beaker, a bar of chocolate and a party at school for the Coronation of George VI. I remember the day well as I ripped my best pair of trousers on a nail and spent a miserable time avoiding the party games and thinking of the retribution that was to come. There was a huge bonfire on the Links on Coronation day and many shops and offices as well as houses displayed flags and bunting. The Italians invaded Abyssinia and we sang silly songs about Mussolini. During the third year at Rockliffe we started to have radio lessons on one afternoon a week, although I can't remember anything about them now. I enjoyed Rockliffe on the whole, had the cane a few times but as ever I was slow and always in the "B" class. I never passed the grading examinations, much to the disappointment of Mr Burnham the 3rd year B teacher, and so returned to Park School in August 1938 – this time in the Senior school.

We were supposed to wear a brown uniform in the senior school but parents bluntly said "no money" and as a compromise the boys were allowed to get away with a cap only. As I hated school caps my mother bought a blazer – through the school – and I paid a shilling a week until it was paid for. The girls mostly wore gym frocks and a little brown hat. There were only seven classes with about forty pupils in each. There were also the woodwork and cookery classrooms with no permanent pupils.

The curriculum was very basic – P.T. (Physical Training) was very evident (there were 2 one-hour periods and 3 half-hour periods per week), a two-hour woodwork lesson on Wednesday and half an hour prayers and scripture lesson every day, leaving only about 12 hours for arithmetic, history, English, geography and general science. There was no homework. However, there were lots of extra-curricular activities – choirs, theatricals etc – and we were all expected to participate in something. I ended up in the choir where we sang "The Lady of Shallot" (which I hated), "The Minstrel Boy" and "Linden Lea" which I loved and can still bring a tear to my eye when I hear it!

There were four "houses", all named after previous headmasters – Wright, Redpath, McQuillan and another whose name I have forgotten. I was in McQuillan and eventually became "captain".

There was no sports field and football, rugby and cricket were all badly organised, but the school excelled in aggressive sports such as boxing, Cumberland wrestling and single stick "fencing", and the houses competed against each other.

There was no talk of School Leaving Certificates or Matriculation, indeed one was taught rather than educated. There was "sums", history never got past the Roman times apart from a few story legends about Alfred the Great, William the Conqueror and Queen Elizabeth I. Geography was either China or South America. I was always sure that we were just being kept off the street and made fit enough to go to war.

There were no school meals and everybody had to go home at lunch time for whatever meal their mother prepared. We always had dinner at lunch time with a high tea later on between 5 and 6 pm. There were no sweet shops near to Park School and the older girls ran a tuck shop where you could buy sweets. I never bothered, having very little money for sweets. My pocket money at the time was 1/3d per week, which went so: 6d for the Monday cinema and 2d for the Saturday afternoon cinema, 3d for the school savings bank (TSB organised), 2d for the cubs and later the scouts, leaving only 2d for sweets. Only Miss Brown, the memory of whom I revere, did anything more to educate rather than drill facts into us. She tried hard to get us to read books, to see "good" films, to have good manners and to have some grooming – much of it in vain I'm afraid. At that time she was the English teacher and I was in her form when war began in September 1939.

At first there was no school at all and parents kept their children at home expecting

the Germans any minute, but later we had to go to someone's house for one hour of lessons per day (and then do homework), but it had to be within 4 minutes of your own home in the event of an air raid. The teachers dashed from house to house. By Christmas 1939 air raid shelters had been built for half of the school population and one week we went in the morning – Saturday as well – and the next week it was afternoons. All extra-curricular activities ceased and indeed over the next two years five teachers departed into the forces. The original woodwork teacher (called up into the 21 years old Militia actually before the war) ended up as a Colonel in the Tank Corps.

Just before the war the King and Queen had been on a North East visit and left for London via Newcastle from Tynemouth station. We were marched from Park School to Tynemouth, had to pay a halfpenny for a paper Union Jack and then played rent-a-crowd for more than an hour on the pretence that we would be presented to their majesties. I dropped my flag and by the time I had picked it up they had swept past in a car. So much for Royalty, I have been a half-hearted republican ever since. We were left to find our own way home which was three miles away with no money.

My schooling virtually finished in 1939, and I learnt more in one winter's night school and a year at the Marine school than in all my previous years. Much knowledge was gained from my cigarette cards.

In the first few days of war, with no school and bored stiff as a result of the new blackout and worrying parents, a few of us found ourselves filling sandbags which were taken and placed in front of the Council Chamber and other notable buildings to protect the entrances and windows from blast. We were doing our bit for the war effort. The bags gradually rotted, the dried sand dribbled out and they were eventually taken away.

The "phoney" war went on until May 1940 and I remember one marvellous weekend on the beach when it could have been peacetime, but then Dunkirk happened and the serious faces returned. One day we sat at our desks and there was no teacher, no Miss Brown. Then she came in, her face white, and told us that France had fallen and that we must be very brave, face the future with resolution etc. It was a speech every bit as good as Churchill's without any writers to help. Then she said the Germans were in Paris and she became very sad (she had been a governess/tutor in Paris); we sat looking at each other not knowing what to do but with the realisation that it was time to gird our loins, toughen our sinews etc – playtime was over.

The school "borrowed" vacant land in Marine Avenue and in Bideford and Cliftonville Gardens for allotments and organised "dig for victory" among the pupils. Tools were bought, but a lot were also donated and we threw ourselves into this activity with enthusiasm. It was run on kibbutz lines and a register was kept of all pupils' times of work. Books were kept of expenditure on seeds etc and eventually on income from sales of produce to the local housewives, school teachers or ourselves. Twice a year the hours were totalled and divided into the profit and all were paid according to the number of hours each had worked. It was perhaps the best education I received at Park School.

The beach cliff tops were sealed off with barbed wire, and several wires stretched over the beach to prevent glider landings and steps to the sand were blown up. You were not allowed to cycle or drive along the promenade at night even with the reduced headlights that were in use. However, there were Sunday night concerts at the Empress, the cinemas opened on Sundays and amusement of some kind became organised to keep the populace happy. I joined the Boy Scouts, khaki drill uniform with badges, stockings with green tabs, scout belt, whistle, scout knife and those wonderful hats (like the Canadian Mounties). We had lots of fun but I also learnt the Morse code, semaphore, how to tie knots and splice ropes long before I went to sea where I had to use all of those skills. We collected aluminium scrap for the war effort.

With the beaches and rocks closed off we went to Hollywell Dene during the rest of 1940, but few fires were allowed (in case they stayed alight after the blackout), the threepenny tins of Heinz beans – with pork – were no longer available to us and the Dene became a lonely place with only a few walkers. In any case we were now more grown up and had bicycles – albeit second-hand – and we were able to go further afield.

CARAVAN CLUB SITE. WHITLEY BAY

Whitley Bay was not an active war place. There were no factories but the army trained men in back lanes etc until a camp was built at what is now the caravan park and the hotels filled with RAF bomber crew on rest leave. There were air raids and Whitley Bay suffered a lot of damage and people were killed. Many more bombs fell in the fields, the more spectacular bombings being on North and especially South Shields. Many lives were lost, particularly at the lemonade factory at North Shields – this was never really reported in the papers, the news just leaked out.

Fear of invasion lessened when Germany turned on Russia and the home front was one of greyness and hard work, with the occasional air raid. I left school at fourteen and a half at Christmas 1941. People still came to Whitley Bay during the war for a few days holiday, mostly to relatives or friends, but it was a trouble with the rationing and they were not popular with the rest of us because they filled the queues for un-rationed foods. I saw a bout of fisticuffs

WINDSOR AIR SERIES WHITLEY BAY
THE NORTH PORTION OF THE BAY

when a housewife berated a visitor – it was in a queue at a fish and chip shop – words were exchanged, the woman went home and returned with her husband (a very big man) who was probably irate at waiting for his supper. The queue had not moved, but the visitor did, nursing some bruises.

There were no photographs taken for picture postcards during the war and in any case you were not allowed to take photos or sketch any buildings or view points. Everyone proudly dashed off to the "portrait studios" to have their picture taken in uniform, but there were no films on sale for your Kodak or Ilford camera. It was not until 1946 that "views" began to appear in the shops for the visitors that were returning to Whitley Bay. There was still rationing and not quite so many houses took in summer visitors, but men were glad to take a holiday in the UK. After all they had been to Africa, Europe and Asia

PROMENADE & CAFE, WHITLEY BAY.

and craved a return to the normality of their memories of pre-war summer holidays with knotted handkerchiefs on heads. Wives longed for a change from the continuing rationing of foodstuffs.

But what of Whitley Bay? It had, grown out from Rockliffe to Davison Avenue, and has been much the same for almost 100 years. Vacant plots have gradually filled in and the old houses in Northumberland Square (behind the Fat Ox) have gone, the old white cottages at the end of Plessey Crescent (it was called Lovers Lane then) vanished to build the new ABC streets Amble, Belsay, Chollerford etc about 1938 and New Whitley in the Quarry also disappeared. So what has changed? Mainly the pace of life. There was little road traffic but plenty of buses and trains. No TV and not many people had the "wireless", we got our Phillips in 1938 and it was magic. Short, Medium and Long waves, Hilversum, Paris, Berlin, Luxemburg as well as Daventry and Stagshaw. Great programmes.

Washing machines were few and far between, it was still poss sticks and tubs, and there were no refrigerators. In truth there was no need for them. My mother did her house chores, making the fire, cleaning the grate, dusting, making the beds and emptying the chamber pots which were still widely used. Very few people had vacuum cleaners but these were becoming more popular. There was no wall to wall carpet, lino with a carpet square or a rug was the norm. These were lifted in spring and beaten in the back lane.

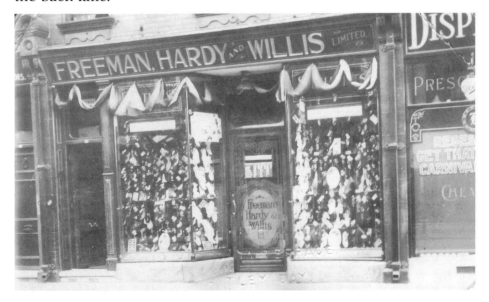

The shopping was a leisurely business and combined getting the food, local knowledge and world news all in an hour or so. In Park View alone we could shop at Duncan's, Maypole, Home & Colonial or Meadow Dairy for groceries. These were all really the same firm, forerunner with

Liptons of Presto and Safeway. There were also better class firms such as Askews, Allards and Walter Wilson's which were local chain store grocers, or single firms such as Keenlysides and Wallers. Greengrocers were Potters and Sampsons. There were lots of good butchers and at least four excellent fish shops. The essentials could be bought within a block and most shops delivered so you did not have to carry large heavy loads.

Whilst doing this you met your cronies, or the shopgirls and men gave out all the news, so all was accomplished. Exercise, service, competition and news. Whitley Bay was a central shopping catchment area for quite a few miles and with the summer visitors there were many really good shops. Ryles and C. Payne for ladies gowns etc, Sorbies, Unsworths and Steels for jewellery, Bullocks and Barrats for cakes, pastries and bread, Thos Hunter's, Hedley & Youngs and that wonderful Mary Russell's for wool and embroidery materials, Eames for pictures and bric-a-brac. All of the shops were good, with many of the staff in a sort of a uniform but all well dressed and nobody needed to go to Newcastle to shop, it was all here in Whitley Bay. Even furniture could be bought at Bainbridges (not the Newcastle JL shop) or the Co-op. If you forgot anything or were too busy there were always the little corner shops which sold everything from butter and bacon to Carters Little Liver Pills. You could also buy bread, cakes, coal, fish, fruit and vegetables in the back lanes from vans or carts and at no extra cost, in fact sometimes cheaper. When I was 13 I delivered groceries for Mr Keenlyside, an old-time grocer, and even though it was wartime and rationing, there were still lots of good things to be had. Most of the staple goods like butter, margarine, sugar and flour were weighed in the back shop. The customer's weekly order was put into boxes then after

school two of us, Ronnie Steel and I, used to take large flat barrows about 5' x 3' and load these up with the boxes and deliver them in an area from Marine Avenue to Monkseaton Drive. The customers were rather snobbish in those days but I was given some 2d and 3d tips and was paid four shillings a week. Later as I became accepted by Mr Keenlyside and his three assistants, I weighed the sugar.

There was also the "home cottage industry" which abounded in prewar days in working class areas. There was always someone who made toffee, either slab (sometimes with coconut on the top) or cinder toffee. There were those who took in washing or ironing and some experts who made clippie or proggy mats and rugs. None of this could pay for the hours of work but the ones who made a name by being good at the work always did a steady trade and it brought in those precious extra pennies.

I had been enrolled for the Marine School at South Shields for a pre-apprenticeship course lasting a year but could not start until I was 15. At first I just stayed at Park School but my friends had left and I became bored so I left at Christmas 1941 and went to work delivering groceries again, from an Allards shop in Eastbourne Gardens. I did not like it, had to use a much overloaded bike and I delivered as far away as the Beehive pub and was forever getting punctures which I had to mend myself and pay for the patches etc. I only stayed for five weeks and then went to work at Rilleys Dairy, delivering milk. This was a good job, well paid (24/- per week), starting at 6 am and finishing by 1 or 2 pm. We – Eddie Shaw and myself – delivered the milk, collected the empties, washed the bottles and filled them; we were left to ourselves and had fun. Later Mr Rilley paid me half a crown extra to collect the money owed by the customers, I enjoyed that nine months and although we had a couple of air raids when bombs were dropped, life went on just the same.

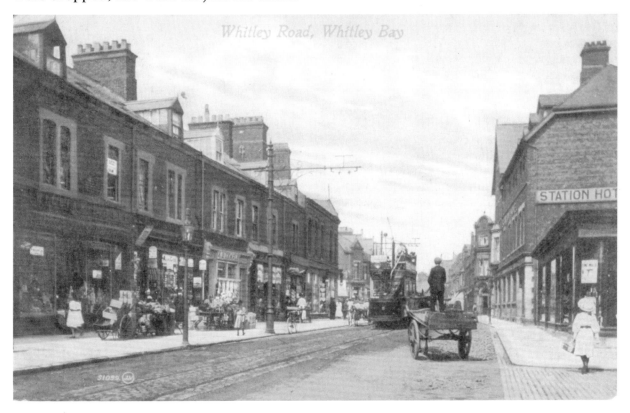

For our holidays Derek Ranson and I went cycling using Youth Hostels, once we even went in a wide sweep down to York and back. We cycled all over the area; the roads were open with very few vehicles, most of them being army. Then in September 1942 I went to the Marine School and started to grow up. My father and I had a walking holiday in the Lake District in June 1943, he had been badly shaken whilst taking shelter in South Shields Market Square when bombs destroyed most of the buildings around him. In September 1943 only three of us at the Marine School had not yet received our apprenticeship papers; we were all accepted by firms but were waiting for our ships, so Brian Ditchburn and myself went cycling in the Lake District. The weather was good and we had an idyllic time in a late summer. By Christmas we were veterans, having gone to sea, been sunk (on different ships!) and been rescued. It was the last holiday either of us had until we both married and had a honeymoon, although we did have leave when our ships docked in the UK.

Somehow the whole tone of living changed when the war started. There was the blackout of course, never a problem for me as I could see well in the dark. The newspapers tried to resurrect the mood of World War I; this was out of date but we became more serious, more grown up. At the same time more effort was made to "have fun while we could" but something was different and you were to some extent hampered by always having to carry your gas mask. Queuing took up time and the gangs and spontaneous fun in the streets seemed to fade away.

Although Whitley Bay was clustered around the area from the church to Woolworth's close to Whitley Hall, there were some odd houses and cottages at other places. The Whitley Bay we know really grew north from Cullercoats, bits here bits there from 1860 on, but from 1880 to 1914 the stretch from Edwards Road to Davison

WHITLEY VILLAGE

Avenue must have been one huge building plot. By 1935 Arcadia were no longer shops of importance, as the central shops and Park View catered for the new homes to the north.

In 1935 there were still two shops in Arcadia with remnants of the iron and glass canopy. I must have worn a millimetre off the window at Storey's pressing my nose against the glass. One side was high class tools, the other side sports. Fishing rods, reels, Webley air pistols and rifles and knives, sheath, Bowie, pen, every type in profusion and

Meccano and Hornby trains. Fabulous Hornbys!

Arcadia and Styan and Helena Avenues were built by the Styan family and this is the only place in Whitley Bay to have the builder's family name. Alf Styan was one of the early builders of that area of Whitley and he and later his son did much of the house building as well as the church at the end of Whitley Road which has only just been demolished. It was a curious church as it had seats like a cinema! The younger Mr Styan lived with his daughter and they were neighbours and family friends of ours – I wish now that I listened more carefully to his tales of old Whitley Bay.

The Methodist church in Victoria Avenue had a direct hit by a bomb in (I think) 1941. Unfortunately two women were killed as they walked along Whitley Road. The Methodists were unlucky as the John Street Methodist church was also destroyed at a later date and a church organist was killed.

You can see the changes which have occurred over the years, in the postcards. The promenade as you can see it today from Rockliffe to South Parade is much as it was in 1935. The pavement area has obviously been widened and parts of the cliff face buttressed against erosion. The last of this work happened about 1950 around the area where the clock is.

Coming north from Rockliffe, Browns Bay was a rather wild and empty place and as the cliffs were crumbling, a defensive wall had to be built. This started in 1939 but then stopped for about fifteen years before it was finished in the late 1950s. Turn round the point and there are the

Table Rocks with swimming pool. Now deserted with a pool which no longer holds much water it is a sorry sight which brings a lump to my throat. Sixty years ago there was no talk of pollution, there were just crowds of people enjoying themselves swimming in water warmed by the sun. I learned to swim there. Competitions were held and lots and lots of people just sat on the rocks and had picnics and watched the swimmers until the tide came in, scattering the swimmers and cleansing the pool. The "Dolphins" had their swimming club changing rooms built against the cliffs and we raced Dinky

toys on the rocks. We fished, caught crabs, dodged the waves crashing onto the rocks and reluctantly went home only half dried after swimming, with our teeth chattering. Sometimes in an evening, when the sun had cast a shadow over the pool and rocks and the crowds had left, we children sailed our toy yachts on the pool. I have never been a strong swimmer but I still recall the excitement and joy when I pushed away from the rock and found myself floundering to the other side, and the shouts of "Mood can swim!" still sound in my head.

It seems strange that only 50-100 years ago you were exhorted to visit the seaside, breathe the air and swim in the healthy briny. Now you are warned not to swim in the polluted seas. I wonder how we will "house-train" the fish and seagulls?

Continuing from Rockliffe there is the lower promenade with the paddling pool, now a very neglected place but in the thirties it was a very popular walking place and for mums who did not wish to risk their children in the sea they could paddle, splash and play in safety. The prom was built around 1930 to tidy up a crumbling cliff face and generally further improve an area which was pleasant. There had been some paths, flower beds and park seats along the cliffs called Victoria Gardens, but these disappeared when the prom was built. There used to be quite a lot of fishing done at high tides. It was still used into the 1960s but not any more.

The Empire Cinema must have been built about 1910 and was later rebuilt – it used to be the most popular cinema, always a full house. It was run by Gaumont British. The Kiddies Club was on Saturday afternoon, twopence downstairs, fourpence upstairs. No adults were allowed. There was a serial – Flash Gordon or Tarzan – a cowboy – Tom Mix, Gene Autrey or Hopalong Cassidy – plus a

CHILDREN'S PADDLING POOL, WHITLEY BAY   21875

couple of shorts – "Our Gang", the Three Stooges, Pete Smith or a sing-along. You had to join the Gaumont British Kiddies Club. It cost nothing and you were given a badge, advance notice of the programmes and – here comes the reason we all joined – a free ticket for three people on your birthday. The manager came out to the foyer, shook hands, wished you a happy birthday and showed you to your seat. Honour indeed, no wonder I have always been a silver screen addict!

All of this part of Whitley Bay was the main Board Residence area. Then the prom widens and becomes the Promenade where crowds just paraded up and down from May to September – it always had lots of people, locals as well as visitors. There was a red cast iron fire alarm on the Promenade opposite Victoria Avenue. I could never understand why it was there, why not in amongst the houses? However, there were very few telephones then and I suppose it could have been reached in an emergency.

The Promenade, Whitley Bay

The two most important hotels were here, the Esplanade and the Waverley. I'm never quite sure if the Waverley was built as an hotel or whether it was houses adapted into a hotel. Whatever, it progressed north from the Esplanade Hotel and built one by one the "towers" which were crenellated, although this false brickwork has now gone. Shortly before World War I the rather grand part of the hotel was built and this, together with the Rotunda, was one of the "picture emblems" of Whitley Bay along with the Lighthouse Logo. The hotel was rather posh in those days; it had its own tennis courts, garages and rooms for the chauffeurs behind the hotels but they were never used to any great extent and there are now flats built on the courts. About 1935 the Waverley obtained a drinks license and changed its name to the Rex so as not to be confused with a chain of temperance hotels called Waverley. Many happy hours were spent on the rocks in front of the hotel. There were several steps to the rocks leading from the paddling pool and the famous corkscrew steps in front of the Rex. These steps were already becoming broken and rusty in the 1930s and they have now gone, although there are new steps nearby from a new concreted area. We used to dare the sea, advancing down the steps as the tide ebbed and eventually made our way out over the rocks to play or fish. I once found a florin; I remember that well as it was four cinema visits or eight Eldorado ice cream tubs!

The "Waverley,"   Whitley Bay, Northumberland.

Over the years the sands have come south over the rocks and then some storm has come along and moved them north again, but usually the sand starts below the clock. During the summer, apart from the weekly boarding visitors there were day trippers most of whom came by train. Some came down Station Road to go to the paddling pool or table rocks, but the majority tracked down Victoria Terrace and South Parade and then down to the lower central prom onto the beach; during the warm sunny days the beach was covered with groups of people. Many brought everything with them, even the teapot to make cups of tea and all they bought was boiling water which many places sold. Apart from the small cafes there was the old-established Greggs Tearoom, it was a cavernous building and provided simple seating and tea and food for many many people. It is now Burnside Lodge after being a furniture shop and flats, but it is still Greggs to me and the slope to the lower prom is still called Greggs Slope.

There were rowing boats for hire at this spot and of course "Fry's Boats" which took lots of people for trips to the lighthouse and back for one shilling. These boats were large cobles with lots of bench seats and one simple mast with a pennant flying, red with the word "Fry" on it. People boarded the boat from small wooden piers which were pushed out on large car or lorry wheels. We tried to help with this on many occasions. I doubt if we helped much but we were tolerated and we pushed and pulled in between building sand castles. At high tide we dared the waves crashing against the paddling pool

prom or raced on the sands from one safe place to another. I lost once and the wave advanced high enough to soak my khaki shorts. I dashed home, let myself in by the key hanging from a string behind the letter box, rinsed my shorts and dried them. Goodness knows what my mother thought but there was a clean pair in the morning and no word was spoken. We left the beach to the crowds and when we wanted to play on the sands we made for the north part of the bay past the lower prom – it was quieter there and we could play out on the small light railway which had been left there years

ago by a ship salvage firm. There were still remnants of this wreck when I was small but it is no longer visible. We dammed streams or built walls of sand against the incoming tide but like old King Canute it was all in vain and nature won in the end.

The lower central prom was a hive of industry until the war. There was – of course – a Maynard's sweet shop and cafes and it was popular except for the south end behind Greggs Slope. At one time there was a Punch and Judy area with small children's seats and for one or two seasons there was a "pierrot" summer show. This may have been tried before, but certainly in 1937 or '38 the council built quite a substantial semi-permanent theatre; the place itself was rather dark, noisy and smelly with the sound of waves at high tide and as the sun went down it was darker and colder so it was not popular. At the northern end of the central promenade was a marvellous "glory hole" run by a scary old woman but who sold all of the usual buckets, spades, windmills, flags, comics, books, sunshades, fishing lines, hooks, sinkers – they were the best and cheapest but it was the one who drew the short straw who went in to buy!

My father and I went out in a boat once from Greggs Slope to catch fish. We caught one, a cod, but Dad had a weak stomach and was promptly seasick; the fish, though fresh, proved more expensive than the shops and I was very disappointed at such a short trip and we never tried it again. Also in 1937 or '38 a speedboat caught fire and was beached off the slope. In no time at all every boy and some girls were swarming over the wreck with hammers etc stripping what was left. I struggled to lift an enormously heavy fly wheel. It proved too much for me and I buried it in the sand. Four boys with their mother's pram came down to collect scrap, saw me hiding the metal and dug it up as soon as I moved away. The four heaved it into the pram where it promptly went through the bottom. Was I ever happy! Serve them right! Next day I returned and pulled and pushed but only got the fly wheel half way up to the lower prom. So I gave up.

PANAMA DIP LOOKING SOUTH, WHITLEY BAY.

In the predominantly fine summers of the late 1930s the beaches were often packed with people and men with huge wickerwork tray baskets wandered around selling sunshades, sunglasses, 4d Sexton Blake novels, buckets, spades – anything to make a tanner. On a good summer's day they found it difficult to walk as the family groups were so close together. This crowd went on to Watts Slope, thinned a little until the Panama Dip and then it was more pleasant with room to play until you reached the end of the lower prom. After that it was empty apart from a few odd groups or walkers.

The Promenade Gardens are now a rather barren area of concrete and grass with some flower beds which do little to attract people to use them but the use of this garden has varied over the years. There used to be many seats and the two wooden

Promenade Gardens, Whitley Bay

shelters, which almost reached their century. There used to be a giant draughts board at the Brook Street shelter (also one at the Rockliffe garden which is now a skateboard "arena") where men played draughts in the summer, moving the pieces with a long stick with a hook on the end. Pre-war the centre of the park was very overgrown with large bushes which were there to hide underground lavatories which had become unsavoury and had been closed for many years since the early 1930s. The backdrop of the Avenue Hotel used to be much nicer than the blank faceless look it has

now; there used to be Oriele Windows and a small wooden gallery which gave it a rather grand appearance.

Back lanes used to be filled with washing. Now unheard of, the practice largely stopped during the war. It was a nightmare on Monday every week; at first light housewives in old houses would light a fire under the copper, others used gas boilers for the hot water and for boiling the whites. Out came the poss tubs and mangles and it was a race to see who pegged out the first sheets and table cloths. Soap powders were Rinso, Oxydol and Persil. Once the clothes were out the women relaxed and exchanged weather comments and gossip. When the bin men, rag and bone men, bakers or grocers or worst, the coal men came into the lane and shouted, what a scurry, as the sheets were taken down or lifted for the vans or horse and carts to get through. Fish were carried in a creel on the vendor's back and he or she used to (hopefully) dodge the washing. Ironing was done in the afternoon; the flat iron had almost gone and we had electric. No plugs, it was fixed into the ceiling light. I used to go to the cinema on a Monday night and everyone was quiet on a Monday. Mothers were a mite tetchy, especially on bad weather days.

The large houses above the Central Prom were high class dwellings, although one end was an ice-cream parlour and there was a newsagents shop, but the Royal Hotel and the Kensington and others were select family holiday hotels. During the war the Royal became The British Restaurant.

28

Ocean View, Charles and Mason Avenue were badly damaged or destroyed in 1941 but otherwise air raid damage occurred only at spasmodic intervals and there had been no air raids or bombs for some time. In August 1943 I was walking along the prom with my father opposite the Willow Cafe and going towards the Rex. The prom was crowded with people; it was a calm late afternoon with a low heavy grey sky. The sudden sound of plane engines startled everyone as it suddenly dropped out of the clouds and its engine roared into life. A soldier walking with his wife or girlfriend turned, as we all did, to watch the plane; he shouted "It's a Heinkel!" and at that moment four bombs were dropped. The plane was not high up; I doubt if it was at more than 500 feet and it was about opposite the Rex. One bomb landed on the John Street Methodist Church which later became a bus garage, enlarged from the old tram garage and has now become a block of flats. I can't remember where the second bomb dropped, the third did not explode and the fourth landed on the Kennersdene Farm near the end of the Broadway (near Holy Cross). I can only think that the pilot was aiming for the anti-aircraft battery on Broadway, because four bombs which were wasted seemed an expensive trip from Germany, but you should have seen the crowd scatter.

PLEASURE GARDENS SPANISH CITY WHITLEY B

The Spanish City pleasure gardens were great fun before the war; perhaps it was because I was so young but it did not seem so garish or tawdry as it did in later life. The gardens which can be seen in some postcards had long gone by 1935. There were the usual dodgems, House That Jack Built (horror and silly mirrors), the Figure of Eight rollercoaster, coconut shies, prove your strength by hitting a pad with a large mallet and sending an object up to ring a bell. This was very popular on a Saturday night when the Territorial Army were at Tynemouth Barracks, showing their prowess to the local girls. There was also "Omar"

SPANISH CITY, WHITLEY BAY   1729

the fortune teller. He and his wife gave "readings". He was a dapper little character with a waxed moustache, cut away collar and frock coat. As soon as he made a bob or two he was off to a local hostelry for a bevy!

The Spanish City is so called because a group of entertainers called the Toreadors held a summer show here in a tent. They came from as far south as Hebburn! Rides have always changed over the years. The Social Whirl, the Joy Wheel and the water chute had already gone by 1935 but the pond was still there and it only vanished when the grounds opened again after the war. Small paddle boats for children went on the water

which was only about 18 inches deep. When the chute closed, next to the Figure of Eight they built the Virginia Reel which lasted until about 1960. This was a violent ride which started about the height of the Figure Eight and descended in a quick and nauseating

THE SOCIAL WHIRL, SPANISH CITY, WHITLEY BAY.

switchback. I only tried it once. I never went on the paddle boats – too tame – I much preferred the competitive stalls like "Joel's Roll-Ups" which gave out huge prizes and half pound blocks of Cadbury's chocolate. The other popular place was the "Scrambler", a helter-skelter with a large bowl of polished maple wood, surrounded on a Friday and Saturday night by all the men who delighted in seeing young girls

Joy Wheel, Whitley Bay

slipping into it. Customers were pulled out by two strong men with ropes who often let go as more people descended into the bowl. Later a small step ladder was built.

I loved it all in the 1930s because of its innocence. I barely noticed local view

postcards – we all wanted to see the McGill type of seaside humour of big-bottomed females. No-one called the Spanish City the "Pleasure Gardens" in fact most kids knew the area as the "White City" from the white coloured Rotunda building. The Empress Ballroom was in those pre-bingo days a dance hall of note, as was the Rotunda Ballroom. The foyer was empty except for yet another Maynard's sweet shop and the north end of this building was made into the Picture House cinema. This was a small but very comfortable cinema, although it was never the most popular cinema, being very exposed to northeasterly weather in the autumn and winter. It was cheap and the programme changed twice or sometimes three times a week. My two sons saw their first film there: *The Three Musketeers*.

Originally the Rotunda had an upper walkway with tea rooms, white columns and partially-glazed areas on either side of the "towers" which had small spheres which complemented the Rotunda. The columns and spheres gave the whole building a more structured appearance and it now looks rather utility to me.

To the left of the Rotunda is what was a

EMPRESS BALLROOM, WHITLEY BAY.

private sea-water baths but this was long gone before we came here and in fact for a time it was a small cinema in the one-reel days. However there was a fire and by 1935 it was "Duncan's Pastimes" a pinball machine arcade.

There was one game in the City called "Simplicity". It was indeed simple but men crowded around this area because side bets were placed – strictly illegal of course, and a watch was kept for the Polis. The whole of the Rotunda building was camouflaged during October-December 1939 as the white dome can be seen for miles.

Whitley Park Hotel was built as one of the large private halls in Whitley Bay. It became an hotel and was then taken over as billets in World War I. I think it must have suffered from neglect during this period although it became an hotel again until it was taken over by the Council to be the chambers and offices when they outgrew the original chambers next to the Victoria Hotel. The park itself was very nice pre-war, being surrounded by a stone wall and wooden railings down Park Avenue. There was a

lodge and the gates were locked at night. The park was varied, with many more trees, a rose garden – with seats – and an open grassed area. At one time there was a small bandstand and an occasional repertory show was given on a temporary stage – I remember "Merrie England".

However, there must have been something wrong with the hall (it was very old) and it was pulled down in 1938 or '39. The council moved into what had been the Priory Cafe at the

bottom of Park Avenue and they remained there until we became part of North Tyneside. The Priory Theatre was next door. This was a World War I wooden hangar taken to pieces and re-erected in the early 1920s. At first there was a substantial brick wall around the building and it was a popular dance hall but the Empress and Rex Hotels were better and it deteriorated to become a roller skating rink with occasional all-in wrestling bouts. After the war it was made into a theatre and rep and in the summer the pierrot shows were held. Other rooms were used as council committee rooms but the whole place was growing old and is now gone and grassed over, and of course the council chambers have gone to Victoria Terrace and Cobalt Business Park. After the hall was demolished the ground was left barren and in 1940 air raid shelters were built for Park School. After the war it became the school canteen. This disappeared and the Public Library car park is there now.

The string of properties behind the park in the illustration below are very old. Originally there was a detached property at the end of the row, which was a nursing home, then a new frontage was erected and it was joined on to the rest of the terrace.

This became the Priory Cafe and later, the council chambers. The large houses at one time had gardens but the widening of roads and paths reduced them to nothing.

The Carlton Cafe seems to me to have been there forever. The Willow Cafe was only built like this about 1937 as there was yet again a vacant plot on the end of these old houses. The

PROMENADE GARDENS, WHITLEY BAY.

last house and the vacant plot became the Willow. On the vacant lot was a white wooden stand that sold limeade, cherryade and saspirella. It was made in a small shed behind the houses and was very frothy and stained your mouth green or red or yellow. The Willow Club was started here in 1938; it was originally just a morning walk for retired men that ended at the Willow Cafe for a cup of coffee. Next was the popular Promenade Club, which is now a pinball machine hall and the club now occupies a house in North Parade. Before the houses continue northward there is a tiny triangle of ground – on this stood yet another wooden shop selling post cards. It used to be very, very popular and lasted almost fifty years.

Bertorelli's ice-cream shop was also here next door to the Promenade Club. The other three great ice-cream parlours were to the north of the Spanish City – The Mecca, then Gallones Venetian ice cream shop (always the best) then the Wonder Bar. They have all gone now as the days of milky coffee and knickerbocker glories have passed, replaced by soft ice cream from a machine. Up to the 1930s some of these houses still had a front garden and Mrs Watts also had her photographic studio here. I bought my first camera at her shop, an Ilford "Selo" folding camera. I saved long and hard; it cost 12/6 and took a 620 eight picture black and white film. Mrs Watts must have been from the same family of the entrepreneur who built the Watts Slope cafe and who also had shuggy boat rides and helter skelters on the sands. I could never understand the story of the women of Cullercoats who manhandled the lifeboat from Cullercoats to Brierdene in about 1850 for a rescue, before good roads were built. Why not launch it from Watts Slope – was it because there was no slope until Mr Watts built, or did they have to get the boat to windward of the wrecked brig? Watts Slope seems to have been

SMITH'S TEA ROOM.

like this for 100 years – a good cafe and the Cullercoats girls for many years sold winkles etc on the slope. When I was small they just had their creels, then old prams were used and eventually small stalls. The small triangle of land opposite the Spanish City, much larger at one time, had a water fountain on it. This was removed to the slope leading to the links where I remember it, and Smith's Tea Room was built here. This was long ago as

THE LINKS   WHITLEY BAY.

road improvements reduced the piece of land and for a long time there was a police box ("TARDIS") here, then a bus enquiry office, but it is now isolated and bare.

The building currently housing the Siam Bay Cuisine restaurant has been an eating place of one type or another for a long time, but used to have a truly elegant exterior with bay windows and lots of ornamental woodwork. It must have been in use as a cafe since Edwardian times. Next door to it there were some political speakers where the Berkeley Tavern is now, but I kept clear of these events not understanding what it was all about.

Leon Dodd's summer show was the great attraction on the Links. The Bandstand has now gone, although the tarmaced area where it stood is still there and its name lives on in the bus timetable. I never did see a band play in it although my grandfather said he had played there around 1899 when he was in the Durham Light Infantry band (flute and piccolo). It was a tiny stage and the artistes must have changed costumes in a space the size of a broom cupboard. The same ones came back year after year, for example the comic Sandy Daws who was in my childhood opinion hilarious. He was the Bobby Thompson sort of comic: bowler hat, dirty mac and always a "tab" in his mouth. His humour was from the school of "a fresh newspaper on the table and fower jam jars, why hinny you've got a tea-set". He did a soft-shoe shuffle and dragged the crowds in. There was the musical

LEON DODD'S "SUPER ENTERTAINERS" (1933)
LINKS BANDSTAND PAVILION   WHITLEY BAY.

couple who sang songs of the light opera – Lehar, Ivor Novello type – and also played the violin. It was a good show and apart from the people sitting on chairs who had paid, the crowds gathered around sometimes ten deep and a collection box was taken round. Over the years seats were arranged and a roof was put up to cover the crowd and canvas curtains to keep out the breeze and to make customers pay to get a seat. The original small metal rail which had gone around the Bandstand was still there and small children climbed over this and sat on a bench to watch the shows. I remember one year a different concert party was on parade but they were not as popular and Leon Dodds came back. They returned after the war and when ocean view was rebuilt they opened the Lenore Guest House, named after their daughter, on the corner with Charles Avenue. She was a member of my class at school; she became a xylophone player and lives in Scotland now, having had some success on stage and radio.

33

The most popular area of the links lay between Watts Slope and the Panama Dip. The tea rooms on Watts Slope were another firm favourite and, like the Panama Dip Tea Rooms, appeared to be built from wrecked ships' woodwork. There were two or three shuggy boat swings on the beach and at one time a helter skelter. Walk a little further north and we are at the Panama Dip, so called because the tea rooms were built from the remains of a ship called the *Panama*, wrecked near Whitley Bay or Cullercoats, and the tearooms boasted very attractive panelling from the ship's cabins. It was a rambling but very attractive and popular place to walk to and partake of afternoon tea. It was there long before the lower prom was built, when the links were still rather wild with gorse bushes and the only buildings around were the Prudhoe Convalescent Homes or farmhouses, and horses and cows grazed on the open ground.

STEPHEN FRY, PANAMA HOUSE, WHITLEY BAY.

The tea rooms were burnt down in 1944 or '45, probably arson, and the event was of sufficient note to be announced on the forces radio in Naples where I happened to be at the time.

The popular terraced garden was built in the dip and at various times there was a small wooden bandstand here, grassed at first but the area is now covered in tarmac. There used to be a windmill near here at one time to pump sea water to the Prudhoe homes for their seawater baths. Later a building was erected to contain a mechanical pump.

CONVALESCENT HOME   Nov. 3rd 1903.   WHITLEY BAY

The Prudhoe Convalescent Home was always a solemn building which was demolished to make way for the Leisure Pool about 1972 but I never saw anyone use the place before the war although I suppose it must have had occupants. During the war it was used by the RAF, as were the Hotels, as a rest and rehabilitation establishment for air crews. The Lodge was occupied by the gardener/caretaker and he grew veggies and sold them from the gardens behind the home.

In 1936 or '37 the Bathing Station was built and a by-law forbidding anyone changing their clothes in public was passed so you had to hire a tent or pay to use the changing rooms. The swimming club also built their rooms which are still there (enlarged in the 1950s).

Bathing Beach, Whitley Bay

To commemorate the 1937 Coronation the drinking fountain was erected on the lower prom. It is not used now of course, as fashions change, but it should be noted as a typical Art Deco 1930s design like many cinemas of that time, late Aztec I call it. The popular attraction here was "Uncle Pat", an evangelist who had a small wooden stage on the sands with a harmonium and who caught his crowds young, with children's talent competitions with a halfpenny toffee bar as the prize. He was there all day and gradually built up the crowds. In the early evening they covered the lower prom and the upper walk as well. He collected pennies from the crowd and eventually built a substantial stage with canvas roof and walls, but a summer storm smashed the lot to matchwood, including the harmonium! He struggled on and regained the popularity as he was a good speaker and held the crowds. A very popular man.

It should be remembered that the "Bay" in Whitley Bay was only added in 1901, because some local who died far away was shipped home for burial but the railway delivered the body to Whitby! Great hullabaloo so we became Whitley Bay, although for a while Whitley-By-The-Sea was used to differentiate from Whitley Chapel. Whitley Road is much as it has been for the last 100 years apart from the trams, which ran from

the ferry to the bandstand. I can remember the lines but the trams were already gone and replaced by buses about 1931. The Ship Hotel was rebuilt about 1926 and the Coliseum facade was built about 1928; it was the other popular cinema in the 1930s, run by ABC (Associated British Cinemas) and was quite opulent with deep pile carpets and well-uniformed usherettes and commissionaire. The Victoria pub has had several frontal changes over the years. The old Council Chambers

remained like this until the mid 1950s when Woolworth's was expanded sideways and heightened for stock rooms. The Regent Terrace side of Whitley Road is much as it ever was apart from changes to shop facias and the trees have gone. The Belvedere corner was created in 1926 by extending a large house with a belvedere tower and part of its conical roof can still be seen on the skyline. The new area contained Sampsons the popular greengrocer and of course the Belvedere pork shop. Before the war they were open until 11:00 or 12:00 at night (at least during the season and at weekends all year) selling hot pork sandwiches – a round bun dipped in hot gravy with lots of pork, stuffing and pease pudding all for sixpence. For a penny you could get a "penny dip" – this was a smaller bun again with gravy and scraps of meat crammed into the bun. It was bedlam trying to get served. They had one rival, Brewis & Watson whose shop was near Boots the chemist on Whitley Road.

I remember the Bus Station being built in 1935/36. There was an old white cottage still there and Arnold Young, a monumental stonemason's yard. When his land was taken over for the station he opened a showroom for gravestones about where Wingers the hairdresser is now and the masonry, carving and sculpting work went to a small works at the top of Edwards Road. I delivered milk to them when I worked for Rilleys Dairy prior to going to sea. They were good blokes and told the best blue jokes whilst carving the headstones.

In 1937 or '38 the Duchess Dene and Briar Dene were prettified with seats and crazy paving paths and the streams controlled. The Links at the north end of the lower prom were also cleared of lots of gorse bushes and the pitch and putt golf courses improved. Revolving chalets were erected in 1937 on the lower prom and had three seasons before the war stopped all seaside activity. They were absent for many years, eventually rebuilt when it was already too late and they have now gone. It was fear of invasion which stopped lots of seaside fun because there were still people who came for a few days holiday. Ice cream was not stopped until 1943 and there were some

amusement arcades open. The Links were open but the beach and lower prom were cordoned off by barbed wire with a gate open twice a day for an hour. There was a searchlight at Curry's Point early in the war, this was a bleak situation for the crew and I am sure it was they who destroyed the breakwater and burnt it for warmth. Early in the war when there was half-day schooling a crowd of us walked to see the searchlight and were rewarded with some brass buttons (Cheshire regiment) as they were now banned for the duration. We also saw a dead German airman being carried off the rocks by four men; I remember he was in a light blue uniform with an Iron Cross ribbon at the throat. We were in high glee as we were convinced he had been shot down by Biggles – "a Hun shot down by an intrepid Biggles doing Immelman turns!". One of the men who looked rather sick told us to shut up and go home. I have often thought of that airman, now of course with remorse, he must have died very young and did not even have much of a war.

Like all seaside resorts, Whitley Bay had the usual publicity stunts which were run by the newspapers. Sand models or sculptures was run by the *Daily Mail*. It needed a good tide and then a fine morning. Officials marked out the clean damp level sand with oblongs about 3x2 and you were only allowed seaweed, shells and small stones for decoration. About a hundred children took part in the competition. I tried twice but never got anywhere near a prize. The other activity was for the grown-ups – a rather obscure picture of someone would be printed and you had to carry a copy of whatever newspaper, approach the person you thought you had identified and say "You are Mr Bloggs and I claim my prize". This gave rise to a lot of embarrassing situations as the photo could fit dozens of people.

SANDCASTLE COMPETITION WHITLEY BAY AUG 19TH 08.

There were several street photographers who operated around the clock and cajoled people into having their photos taken. I bought and kept several. There was one really old-fashioned photographer for whom you had to pose (the others-were 'action' shots) whose photographs were on "tin plate" and were instant. He had a rubber bag hanging on his tripod and this held a "fixer" which printed the picture. They were rather dark pictures and just a novelty – a late use of Daguerreotypes. There was also the "comic" photo shop near the Picture House cinema at the Rotunda where you either stick your face through a hole in a "saucy" painted pose or there was also the garden bench with a long aspidistra for a more serious picture. I think this was a Jerome shop, one of a chain of photograph portrait shops all over Britain.

WINDSOR AIR SERIES
WHITLEY BAY   FROM ST. MARY'S LIGHTHOUSE

The history of the lighthouse is well documented; built about 100 years ago, the light was originally a paraffin fuelled Mantle light which was visible for 17 miles. The keeper's house had a flat roof – was this to catch rain water? A pitched roof was added after the war. The paraffin light had to be attended to frequently and was replaced with electric lamps as these became more reliable.

Race week in June used to be a much more important local event, together with the Hoppings on the Town Moor. The Northumberland Plate (Pitman's Derby) was held on a Wednesday. Schools had the whole week off as a holiday and many large firms, the shipyards and the pits gave Wednesday afternoon off as so many left for the Race. The jockeys used to come to Whitley Bay to ride the beach donkeys at the Rockliffe Rugby Club ground at Hillheads. It was called the "Donkey Derby", all for charity and great fun, and was really the start of the summer season. The Quarry in those days was banned to the public as it was a reservoir of water for the Tynemouth Water Company. It was overgrown and to deter us kids the water was rumoured to be bottomless and there were ferocious Alsatians loose in the woods. We all dared each other to enter, which we did and then scurried out. There were street carnivals in the early

Donkeys on the Sands. Whitley Bay.

1930s. I can't remember that this happened every year but it was obviously to drum up trade. Local merchants decked out their lorries and horse and carts. At seven years old I thought it was very exciting. There was also some attempt at illuminations come September and the darker nights, but it was not on a very large scale.

Whitley Public Library did not open until September 1939 (officially opened January 1940). I joined on the second day it opened so I must be getting on for an original member. It became the Sands night club when the library was built in the park. Opposite the bus station and Post Office were shops which were demolished to make way for the Presto supermarket. There were butchers, bakers, a ladies clothes shop, Teasdale's dairy, a great sweet shop, all with flats over them, and that den of iniquity the billiards room, which all lasted until the late 1960s.

Before the Public there was Boots library, although I never used it as I could not understand why a chemist had books for hire or indeed why they should be a chemists at all – I always thought they should sell shoes. About 1937 the Silver Library opened, it cost two pence to borrow a book for a week. They had a children's section with all of the "William" books, Percy F. Westerman, Biggles etc – I read the lot. I really enjoyed that library. It remained long after the Public Library opened, eventually moving to another shop in Park View and then disappeared. Another library opened at the top of

Monkseaton Village.

Victoria Avenue, which was owned by a man who also loaned out gramophone records. I never saw a lot of people there however; it was just not in a popular shopping area and soon disappeared when the war started.

Although I rarely went to Monkseaton, I

was in St Peter's cubs for a couple of years and went to the corrugated iron church hall in Chapel Lane, which together with the simple church was where
St Peter's was situated until the present church was built. There were swings etc where the footbridge is and of course there were the ramps at Monkseaton Station. This was all under glass, so was dry on a wet day and was one of the best race tracks for Dinky cars. Not the ramp on the west side as this had a ticket collector at the foot! You could set off your Dinky car and then race down the slope to prevent it going under the barriers. Souter Park was only about 10 or 15 years old then and was very popular for bowls and especially tennis. There were some very good players who were all dressed in their long white flannels and the girls, whose "short"

SOUTAR PARK, WHITLEY BAY.

dresses were much longer than current fashions. They played strictly to the rules and had lots of spectators on a warm summer evening.

I was growing up, times were different and although like everywhere else Whitley Bay had tried to resume its pre-war splendour, when everyone wanted to return to home and normality; it has now become a dormitory town and the seaside town has largely disappeared. Perhaps some new entrepreneur will come along to resurrect the potential which is here, but we will need to have those wonderful sunny summers of 1935-1940 when the sky and sea were blue and everyone enjoyed themselves, when everyone was HAVING A WONDERFUL TIME AT WHITLEY BAY.

IT'S O.K. HERE HAVING A FINE TIME! Something to crow about! Whitley Bay